LIBRARIES NI
WITHDRAWN FROM STOCK

KU-168-072

VICTORIAN BELFAST

419529

Published 1993
by the Ulster Historical Foundation
Balmoral Buildings
12 College Square East
Belfast BT1 6DD
Northern Ireland

All rights reserved. No part of this publication may be reproduced, stored in a retrieval system
or transmitted in any form or by any means, electronic, mechanical or otherwise, without the
prior permission of the publisher.

The Ulster Historical Foundation gratefully acknowledges the financial assistance of **Belfast
City Council** with the publication of this book.

This book has received financial assistance under the **Cultural Traditions Programme** which
aims to encourage acceptance and understanding of cultural diversity.

© Jamie Johnston and the Ulster Historical Foundation 1993

ISBN 0 901905 57 7

Printed by the Universities Press
Alanbrooke Road, Belfast.

Design by Wendy Dunbar

Cover Illustration: Map of Belfast, c.1865 reproduced by kind permission of the Trustees of
the Ulster Museum.

PREFACE

8 8 ? ? ? ?

This booklet concentrates on the industrial development of the city of Belfast during the 19th century. It is designed to provide class work for one term and would be suitable as either a study in depth or a local study at Key Stage 3.

It should be emphasised that the exercises at the end of each chapter are suggestions. Teachers are encouraged to develop further exercises in line with the attainment targets as stipulated in the History programme of study.

The permanent exhibition at the Ulster Museum, 'Made in Belfast', is complementary to much of this course. The Museum welcomes school trips to the exhibition and can provide activity sheets and illustrated talks. A range of other classroom materials is in the course of preparation.

For further information regarding school visits, talks and other teaching materials, contact the Education Officer at the Ulster Museum. A number of sources are to be found in the Public Record Office of Northern Ireland. Teachers who are interested in obtaining additional sources, or information about sources, are encouraged to make contact with the Public Services section of PRONI.

ACKNOWLEDGEMENTS

My thanks are due to a number of people and official bodies without whose support it would not have been possible to complete this textbook: the Headmaster and Board of Governors of Glengormley High School and the Department of Education (N.I.) for supporting my secondment to the Public Record Office of Northern Ireland for one year; to the staff of PRONI, particularly the Public Search Room staff for their help and forbearance throughout the year and Trevor Parkhill for his patience and continued interest in this project; to the Deputy Keeper of the Records for permission to reproduce illustrations; to Tony Crowe for his wit and wisdom throughout the year and, finally and most importantly, to my wife Margaret, for her enthusiasm and encouragement throughout the research and writing of this book.

The publisher acknowledges the help of the following: Dr Vivienne Pollock of the Ulster Museum for help in identifying suitable illustrations; the Public Record Office in London for permission to reproduce the map of Belfast in 1570 on pages 2-3; the Linenhall Library for permission to reproduce the plan of the *Grecian and Italian* ship on page 26; the Deputy Keeper of the Public Record Office of Northern Ireland and Lamont Holdings Plc for permission to reproduce the illustration of Belfast Ropeworks on page 34; the Director of the Public Record Office of Northern Ireland for permission to reproduce the illustrations on pages 5, 6, 16, 17, 18, 22, 23, 29, 30 and 31; the Ulster Folk and Transport Museum for permission to reproduce the illustration on page 10. The illustrations on pages 7, 9, 20, 25, 38, 41, 44, 48, 49, 51 and 55 are reproduced by kind permission of the Trustees of the Ulster Museum.

CONTENTS

BELFAST UNTIL 1800

'THE SANDBANK'

According to P. W. Joyce (*Book of Irish Names*, Belfast, 1990), the name Belfast derives from two Gaelic words — *beol* meaning a ford and *fearsad* meaning a sandbank. A ford is a crossing point of a river.

The crossing point of a river has always had great strategic importance because whoever controlled the crossing point also had power over the surrounding countryside. This explains why the Norman knight John de Courcy, who invaded Down and Antrim in 1177, built a castle at Belfast. Now he could defend South Antrim from the attacks of the Irish clans of North Down by stationing a few men to control the ford at Belfast from their simple castle.

No evidence of this first castle survives so we can conclude that it was a less permanent structure than de Courcy's great castle at Carrickfergus. However, from this time onwards, there does appear to have been some castle at Belfast to control this crossing point between North Down and South Antrim. However, there is very little evidence of other buildings in the area at this time. Belfast was not to grow into a town for another 400 years.

Belfast was probably one of the castles captured by Edward Bruce in 1316. Indeed, the castle appears to have changed hands several times over the years, again emphasising its strategic importance. Evidence exists to show that the castle was captured in 1476, 1489, 1503, 1512 and 1523.

The map of Belfast Lough dated 1570 is the earliest known map of this area and clearly shows Belfast as little more than a castle built to defend the river crossing.

Look at the map carefully and answer the questions which follow.

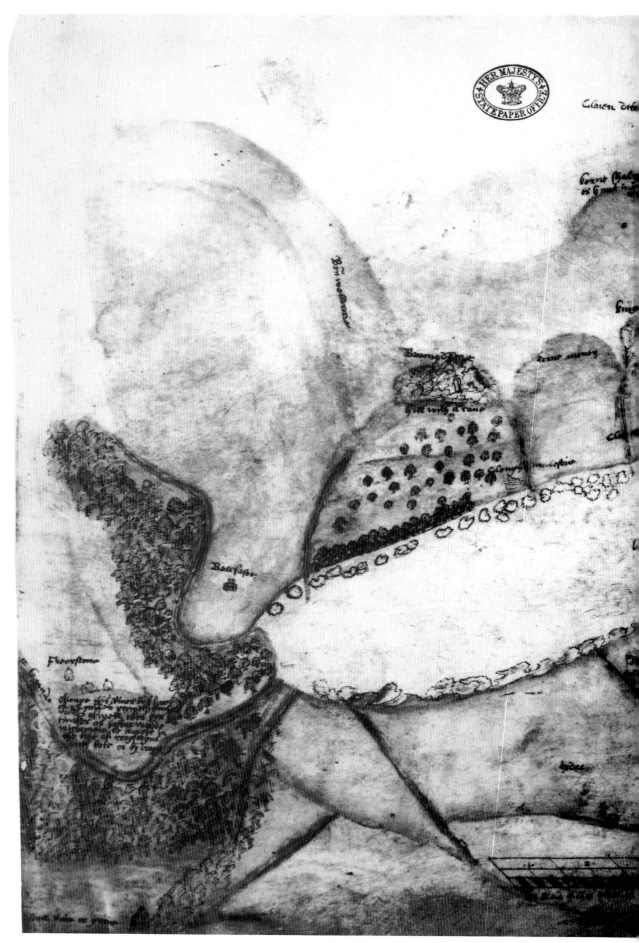

First known Chart of

Public Record

Lough, about 1570

ndon, MPF 77.

Learning activities

Q1   (a) How is Belfast spelt on the map?

        (b) What buildings are shown at Belfast according to the map?

        (c) Are there any other buildings near Belfast shown on the map?

        (d) What does this map tell us about the size of Belfast in 1570?

        (e) What was the countryside around Belfast like according to the map?

        (f) Where was the main port in Belfast Lough according to the map?

        (g) Do you recognise any further features on this map?
            Write down all the features which you recognise.

LOOK BACK AT THE TEXT

Q2   **Write out the following sentences and fill in the gaps.**

        (a) In English, *beol* means _____.

        (b) In English, *fearsad* means _____.

        (c) A ford is a type of _____ _____.

Q3   (a) Who built the first Belfast castle?

        (b) Name one other famous castle built by this man.

Belfast begins to grow

The plantation of Ulster, which began at the start of the 17th century, saw the beginning of the growth of Belfast into the largest town in Ulster.

In 1604, the town, manor and castle of Belfast were granted to Sir Arthur Chichester, Lord Deputy of Ireland. Chichester immediately ordered that the castle at Belfast should be repaired as it had been badly damaged in the conflicts of the previous century.

The Plantation Commissioners' Report of 1611 records:

*We came to Belfast where we found many masons, bricklayers and other labourers...
had taken down the ruins of the decayed castle.*

The Plantation Commissioners' Report then continues to tell us where these labourers etc. had come from.

The town of Belfast (has) many families of English, Scottish and some Manxmen already inhabiting... who have built good timber houses with chimneys.

This provides evidence of the plantation of Ulster taking effect.

In 1613, Belfast was granted a charter by King James I. The town became a municipality with the right to elect a mayor, 12 burgesses (councillors) and send 2 M.P.s to Westminster.

Belfast continued to grow throughout the 17th century. There was as yet very little manufacturing activity in Belfast. There was a small brickworks which provided materials for local buildings but attempts to set up an iron foundry had failed. Instead, Belfast prospered by acting as a market place for the farmers of the Lagan valley and surrounding countryside and exporting their produce by sea to other parts of Ireland or across the sea to England and Scotland.

By the end of the 17th century, Belfast had clearly replaced Carrickfergus as the most important port in Ulster and was handling 5 or 6 times more trade than Carrickfergus. The list of imports and exports passing through the port of Belfast shows the importance of farming in Ulster at this time and the lack of any industry or local mining (see next page for table of exports).

Exports	Imports
beef	coal
butter	cloth
hides	wine
tallow	brandy
corn	paper
	timber
	tobacco

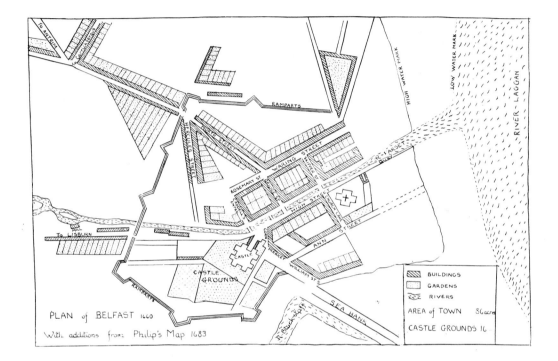

Plan of Belfast 1660, with additions from a map of 1683.
PRONI T2456.

Plan of Belfast 1660, with additions from a map of 1683. Study this map carefully and answer the questions which follow.

Learning activities

Q4 According to the map of Belfast in 1660:

(a) What was the size of the town?

(b) Did the town of Belfast have walls?

(c) Where was Belfast Harbour?

(d) Why could you get your feet wet in High Street?

(e) Why do you think the following streets got their name:
Bridge Street, Church Lane, Skipper Street, Corn Market.

LOOK BACK AT THE TEXT

Q5 (a) Write out the phrase in the Plantation Commissioners' Report which tells us that the old castle was in ruins by 1611.

(b) The evidence of the Plantation Commissioners mentions three places from which families have come to settle in Belfast. What are they?

Q4   Look at the list of imports and exports.
  (a) *One* animal connects *four* of these exports. Which animal?
  (b) Name two types of farming popular in the Lagan Valley at this time?

Q5   Look back to the map of 1570.
  Why is it surprising that the people of Belfast had to import timber by the end of the 17th century?
  What must have happened in the 100 years between 1570 and 1670?
  Can you think why this change took place?

The 18th century

The 18th century saw only gradual growth in the town of Belfast. The main role of the town, as a market place and port which served the surrounding countryside, continued. Indeed this role increased with the development of linen production in the Lagan Valley. The building of the White Linen Hall in Belfast in 1785 emphasised how important this trade had become to the commercial life of Belfast during the century.

Apart from its commercial life, Belfast enjoyed a reputation as a liberal town where much discussion of political and religious matters took place. Evidence of a literate and educated population can be found in the fact that the oldest surviving daily newspaper in the world is the *Belfast News Letter*, first published in 1737. The founding of the Belfast Academy (today called Belfast Royal Academy) in 1785 and of a Belfast library, later to be called the Linenhall Library, in 1788 also provide evidence of an educated, literate and inquiring population.

Alongside this educated and generally well-off class there was, of course, the poor. Here again the educated classes played their part by establishing the Belfast Charitable Society in 1752 and building the Poor House by 1774.

However, as the illustration of Belfast in 1792 shows, Belfast was still by the end of the 18th century a small town by the standards of today. The population of the town by 1801 was only 19,000, industry was still practically non-existent and hopes of improving the port had become bogged down in the sandbank to which Belfast owed its name. The transformation of the town over the next 100 years was to be dramatic.

Belfast in 1792.
PRONI D1105/7.

Study this illustration of Castle Place and High Street in Belfast in 1786 carefully and answer the questions which follow.
Ulster Museum IC/High St/786.

Learning activities

Q7   (a) Are there any differences between High Street in 1786 and High Street in the map of 1660?

      (b) Where is the harbour in this illustration?

      (c) Look carefully at the buildings in the illustration.
How many stories have most of the buildings?
Do they have thatched roofs?
Many of the buildings have signs hanging outside. Does this suggest they were houses or shops?

      (d) Look carefully at the road.
Was the road paved or tarred?
Was there a pavement?
What different activities are going on in the road?
What animals are shown on the road?

      (e) In the illustration the road looks very clean. Do you think it would really have looked like this? Explain your answer.

LOOK BACK AT THE TEXT

Q8   Under a heading *BELFAST UNTIL 1800* draw a timeline showing the major events in the history of Belfast from 1100 to 1800. Use a scale of 1cm.=50 years.

Q9   Using both the text and the timeline, write down a list of what you think are the most important changes which have taken place between 1200 and 1800?

Q10 Which of the following people had the greatest impact in encouraging these changes:

      (a) John de Courcy

      (b) Sir Arthur Chichester

      (c) Businessmen of the 18th century

      Pick only one and give at least one reason for your choice.

HISTORY OF LINEN MANUFACTURE

Linen has been produced in Ireland for many centuries. Until the 19th century, the production of linen was a cottage industry. This means that linen was produced at home by farmers and their families.

The farmer would grow some flax on his land. His wife and children would then prepare and spin the flax into linen thread and, finally, the farmer would weave the thread into cloth on a hand loom. The farmer would then sell the cloth to bleachers and, in this way, would earn extra money for the family.

The demand for Irish linen was always high because of the fine quality of the cloth produced. The bleachers of the Lagan Valley built up close links with markets in England and began to export their cloth to England via Belfast rather than Dublin. The White Linen Hall was built in Belfast in 1785 to organise the trade and shipment of linen to England. This seemed to emphasise the fact that the centre of the linen trade was moving north into Ulster.

The cotton industry in Belfast

However, the first mills to be built in Belfast at the start of the 19th century were cotton mills, not linen mills. At this time, spinning linen by machine posed too many problems.

Cotton spinning reached its peak in Belfast in 1826 when over 3,500 people were employed in 20 mills. However, about this time a trade barrier, which had protected the Belfast cotton industry from the competition of the Lancashire cotton industry, was removed. The cotton industry in Belfast went into decline.

The linen industry becomes industrialised

Two events came to the aid of the Belfast textile industry. Firstly, in 1825, James Kay of Preston discovered a method which allowed linen to be spun successfully by machine. Then, in 1828, a fire destroyed Mulholland's Cotton Spinning Mill on Henry Street.

Mulholland turned the disaster of the fire into an opportunity to investigate the possibility of using Kay's process of spinning flax into linen. An experiment in 1828-29 using 1000 flax spindles worked successfully. When Mulholland built his new mill in York Street in 1830, it was built only for flax spinning.

Mechanisation had come to the linen industry and Belfast had discovered an industry in which it could lead the world. Mulholland's example was soon followed by other mill owners. By 1850, there were 29 mills in Belfast spinning flax and only 4 mills spinning cotton.

Weaving the thread into cloth was still done by hand at this time. The great power looms could only produce rough linen cloth, not the fine linen demanded by customers in England and elsewhere. In any case, the wages for weavers were so low that the linen manufacturers saw no reason to spend money on machines when labour was so cheap.

It was not until the 1850s that weaving became mechanised. The effects of the Great Famine (1845-49) and emigration had greatly reduced the numbers of weavers. Those weavers who were left began to demand higher and higher wages for their work.

Faced with these rising costs, the mill owners now turned to power looms. Due to recent developments power looms could produce much better quality linen. Only the very finest linen still had to be woven by hand.

Belfast — linen capital of the world

By the 1860s, therefore, the linen industry was fully mechanised. Then came another piece of good luck for the linen industry and bad luck for the cotton industry. Across the Atlantic, the American Civil War began.

During this war, the American northern states blockaded the ports of the southern states. As a result, the raw cotton needed by the Lancashire cotton industry could not get to England. The cotton industry went into a temporary decline and the demand for cloth was met by linen. Belfast experienced a boom and the number of spindles used in spinning linen thread increased from 500,000 in 1862 to 724,000 in 1868. In the same period the number of power looms increased from 3000 to nearly 9000.

J. N. Richardson Sons and Owdens Linen Warehouse, 1861.
Ulster Museum W10/21/116.

The end of the American Civil War and the restoration of cotton supply marked the first setback for Belfast's linen industry. Firms which had borrowed too much money in expectation of high profits found themselves unable to sell enough linen to pay their debts. They fell into bankruptcy and mills had to close.

Such bankruptcies and mill closures occurred in 1875 and again in 1897-98. However, it would be wrong to consider these periods as times of major setbacks for the linen industry. Rather, they were due to the miscalculations of businessmen overstretching their finances. In 1910, linen was still one of the two biggest industries in Belfast and both employer and employee were looking forward to many years of continued work and prosperity.

Belfast truly was 'Linenopolis' — the linen capital of the world.

Learning activities

Q1 Draw a timeline called 'The History of Linen Manufacture'. The timeline should show all the main events in the development of the linen industry between 1750 and 1900. Use a scale of 1cm.=10 years.

Q2 Write a sentence explaining what is meant by the phrase 'cottage industry'.

Q3 Write a list of the inventions which caused the linen industry to change from a cottage industry into a factory industry.

Q4 Write down any examples of chance — either good luck or bad luck — playing a part in this story.

Q5 Why did Belfast businessmen change from manufacturing cotton to linen?

Q6 What events outside Northern Ireland helped the growth of the linen industry in Belfast? Explain carefully how each event helped.

Q7 Look back at the answers to your last four questions. All of these answers list the things which helped or encouraged change in the Belfast linen industry. These are called FACTORS OF CHANGE. Now list these factors under the headings:

(a) Economic

(b) Social

(c) Political

Explain the reasons for your choice.

HOW LINEN WAS MADE

In the field

Flax was often grown on land which had been used to grow potatoes. The plant was sown in April and was ready to be harvested by late July or August. The plant was pulled out by the roots, not cut, as the fibre, which was the part of the plant used to make the thread, went down into the roots.

The next stage was called retting or rotting. The idea was to rot the woody interior of the plant and allow the flax fibre to be removed easily. To do this, the flax was tied into bundles, submerged into shallow ponds of water, weighed down and covered with straw.

Putting flax into the lint-dam.
Ulster Folk and Transport Museum WAG 1013.

After 7 to 10 days, the flax was taken from the ponds and grassed, i.e. exposed to the air. This helped to make the separation of fibre and wood easier. The flax was now ready for scutching. A scutching machine would beat the flax stalks, separating fibre from wood.

In the mill

The flax was now ready to go to the spinning mill. However the fibres were still too thick and rough for spinning. Yet more preparation was required before thread could be produced.

The first job in the mill was roughing. This entailed sorting, cleaning and arranging the fibre as it arrived from the scutching mill. The fibres were separated as much as possible and sorted into groups of roughly equal length.

The fibre was now ready for the hackling machines which further separated the fibres and combed them to the required degree of fineness. By the time this process was finished, the flax fibre was soft and glossy.

The fibres were now sorted according to quality and length, put through a spreading machine and drawn until they finally had the appearance of thread. In the roving room this fine clean fibre was put onto a spindle ready for the spinning machines.

From thread to cloth

Once the thread was spun it was changed from bobbins to reels in the reeling room to prepare it for weaving. In the winding room, the thread was further prepared for the power looms. The weft thread (cross threads) were put on to bobbins and the warp threads wound on to spools. The threads were then dressed by applying an adhesive substance to the threads which gave added strength to the finished cloth.

After weaving, the linen was still not finished. The cloth was still rough to the touch and a dirty brown colour. Now the linen had to be *bleached* either on the bleach greens of the Ulster countryside or, and more likely as the century progressed, by a chemical process until it acquired a pure white colour. It then went through a process called *beetling* in which the cloth was pummelled by wooden blocks in a machine, flattening and closing up the threads and softening the material at the same time.

Finally the linen was ready for the finishing rooms where it would be embroidered and packed ready for shipment to England and around the world.

Learning activities

Q5   Here is a list of some of the jobs involved in the making of linen:
   (a) Beetling
   (b) Bleaching
   (c) Dressing
   (d) Hackling
   (e) Reeling
   (f) Retting
   (g) Roughing
   (h) Scutching
   (i) Spinning
   (j) Weaving

The jobs are listed in alphabetical order. Sort them into the correct order in which they occur when making linen.

Now write a sentence describing each job.

THE MILL WORKERS

The linen industry transformed Belfast from a market town and port into one of the great cities of the United Kingdom. The linen merchants and mill owners became very wealthy people, building grand houses on the outskirts of the city and enjoying all the privileges of great wealth.

However, the mill workers did not share in this great wealth and prosperity and their experiences show another side to the story of the growth of Belfast.

Working conditions

HOURS

The workforce in the mill consisted mainly of women and children. This was because women and children were cheaper to employ and were less likely to complain about the terrible conditions under which they worked.

The age at which children could begin work was controlled by law. The minimum age for starting work in the mill was 10 years in 1874, 11 years in 1891 and 12 years in 1901. These juveniles or 'half-timers' attended school either in the mornings or afternoons or on alternate days. By the time they were 14 they could work full-time in the mill.

However, some parents were so keen to get their children into work and earning money that lies were often told about a child's age. Many children started work a year or more before the law would allow.

Hours of work in the mill were long. Work started at 6.30am and finished at 6.00pm. Workers were given 45 minutes for breakfast and 45 minutes for lunch. Rules of the mill regarding lateness for work or poor work were very strict and fines were greatly feared by the workforce.

WAGES

Wages in the mill were not good. Indeed, the low rate of pay in Belfast mills was one of the reasons why linen remained so competitive on the world market. Compared to the textile workers of England, the workers of Belfast were poorly paid.

The following table gives some idea of prices at the time and wages paid in the mills.

In 1855
4lb. loaf cost 3p.
1lb. meat cost 2 $\frac{1}{2}$p.
1cwt. coal cost 3p.
Women and girls were paid 27 $\frac{1}{2}$p. per week
Boys were paid 16p. per week
Unskilled men were paid 52 $\frac{1}{2}$p. per week

By 1905 there had been some improvement:
4lb. loaf cost 2 $\frac{1}{2}$p.
1lb. meat cost 2 $\frac{1}{2}$p.
1cwt. coal cost 4p.

Women and girls were paid 45p. per week
Boys were paid 50p. per week
Unskilled men were paid 85p. per week

It has been estimated that an unskilled man could earn just enough to keep a family of a wife and two children with 'minimum comfort'.

Reasons for low wages

Why were the wages so low in Belfast? There are several answers to this question:

1   The unskilled nature of the work.

2   There was a constant pool of unemployed labour in Belfast who were willing and able to do the work if those in work complained and went on strike.

3   Most of the workers were women and children who were traditionally paid less than men.

4   Trade Unions were very weak in the Belfast textile industry. By 1910 less than 12% of workers were in a union.

5   As a result, the workers in the mills rarely attempted to challenge the employers. On the occasions that they did the results were not encouraging.

    1872 - roughers and sorters went on strike for 5 weeks asking for a 20% rise in wages - STRIKE FAILED

    1874 - 43 mills went on strike after employers imposed a cut in wages - STRIKE FAILED

The striking workers were simply replaced by other workers from outside or else by machines.

It should be noted however that skilled workers and overseers in the mills were quite well paid for that time and indeed could aspire to a good standard of living. These senior jobs were always filled by men.

1855	Skilled man	- 90p per week
	Overseer	- £1.20p per week
1905	Skilled man	- £1.15p per week
	Overseer	- £2.10p per week

Learning activities

Q6   How many hours a day did a mill worker have to work? Remember not to count the time off for breakfast and lunch.

Q7   In the chapter, there are prices for bread, meat and fuel.
Make a list of the other things a family would have to spend money on.
What kind of things could a mill-working family probably not afford.

Q8   Write down 4 reasons why wages were so low.

Q9   Why do you think the strikes in 1872 and 1874 failed?

Health

During the 19th century, the employers and mill owners were interested in producing as much linen as possible and selling the linen at a good profit. They did not consider the effect of working in the mills on the health of their workers.

By the end of the 19th century, however, local doctors and factory inspectors were complaining about conditions in the mills and how the workers were affected. The following information comes from these reports.

Roughing, hackling and carding

In these departments the main problem was the dust given off by the flax. This dust was called 'pouce'. Continually breathing the fine dust or pouce led to all manner of chest complaints. A worker would be liable to take a violent coughing fit — the other workers then said he was 'poucey' — and double over, grabbing hold of anything to steady himself. The violent coughing spasms were in fact early signs of a type of tuberculosis called phthisis. The army surgeons of the period were aware of this and had forbidden their recruiting sergeants from enlisting any men who worked in these departments of the mill.

In the carding room, where the workforce was nearly all girls, the atmosphere was also very dusty and accidents with the carding machines quite horrific. One example was reported in the *Belfast News Letter* on 1st May 1854 and referred to a mill worker called Sarah Jane Quinn:

> *She was engaged at the carding part of the machinery and her head by some means got entangled in the machinery in which the greater part of the scalp was removed from the head and the skull was severely injured. She was conveyed to hospital but little hope was entertained of her recovery.*

A survey, carried out in 1872, discovered that the average working life for someone in these departments was 16.8 years and that 31 out of every 1000 workers died each year. In 1891, it was found that nearly half of the linen workers in Belfast suffered from phthisis and that 90% of these were under 40 years old.

Spinning

The spinning rooms had their own special problems. Here the workers were nearly all female and they were forced to work in warm and wet conditions. Their problems were described by Dr Purdon:

> *Another department that has a peculiar disease called by the workers 'Mill Fever' is the spinning. This generally attacks raw hands and comes on when they are at work a few days. The symptoms are rigors, nausea, vomiting, quickly followed by pain in the head, thirst, heat of skin &c. This state continues from two to eight days, when the disease subsides itself. No treatment is required or sought for, as the worker knows that it runs a certain course and will leave her comparatively well, though weak and that she may return to work without any dread of having it again. The cause assigned for the attack is the smell of oil, along with the vapour and heat of the room.*

> *The spinners suffer from oedema of the legs and ankles; also from varicose veins and, on each Monday morning, after being in for a short time, many of them become so faint and giddy that they are obliged to go out into the lobbies in order to recover themselves.*

In another factory inspector's report, it was stated that children who worked in mills in Belfast had poorer stamina and were smaller than those who worked in the cotton mills of England.

Weaving

The weaving rooms were also hazardous to health. Again, these rooms had to be very humid. Indeed they were so humid that evaporation from the body would stop with the result that body temperature would rise and this would lead to giddiness and general drowsiness. Again in such conditions, chest diseases were common.

Bleaching

The chemicals used in the bleaching departments of the mills also caused problems. Dr Purdon reported:

> *Those engaged in bleaching yarn... suffer from an attack of Eczema of the hands and fingers of so severe a character that fissures are formed which bleed frequently. The disease commences in about twenty-four hours after commencing to work, and in two or three days the pain is so great that they have to stop until the parts are healed.*

Learning activities

Q10 Copy out the following paragraphs and fill in the gaps:

HEALTH IN THE MILLS

The roughing, h_____ and carding departments were filled with a fine dust called p_____. This pouce caused the workers to c____ violently, sometimes leading to a _____. Eventually, the fine dust could cause c_____ d_____ such as phthisis.

The spinning rooms were very w____ and w____. This led to a strange disease which the mill-workers called m_____ f_____. Factory inspectors said that c_____ who worked in the mills in Belfast were s_____ than children who worked in mills in E_____.

Weaving could also lead to c_____ d_____ and skin problems were caused by the c_____ used in the b_____ department.

The nicest place to work in the mill was in the w_____ as here the a_____ was clear and bright.

Q11 Divide into groups of four.

(a) Read the information on housing and diet. Make a list of all the problems concerned with the houses and the poor diet.

(b) Make a list of all the health problems concerned with working in the mills.

(c) Imagine you are a group of factory and health inspectors in the 19th century. Make a list of all the improvements you would like the mill owners to make to improve conditions for the mill workers.

(d) Nominate a spokesperson for your group. Each spokesperson will then report to the rest of the class the improvements demanded by your group. Make a list of the most popular suggestions on the blackboard.

(e) Return to your group. This time you are a group of mill owners deciding how to react to the improvements demanded by the inspectors. Make a note of any objections you have to the suggested improvements. Select a new spokesperson and report back to the rest of the class.

(f) Write in your workbook both a factory inspector's report on a Belfast mill and the response from the mill owner. Each piece of work should be about one page in length.

Warerooms

In fact, the only part of the mill which seems to have been relatively free of health problems were the finishing rooms. Here the atmosphere was clear and bright, the finished linen clean and crisp. As a result, the workers in the finishing rooms saw themselves as very superior to the workers in the rest of the mill. Indeed, they claimed not to work in a mill at all but insisted in calling it a wareroom.

Housing and diet

The houses provided for the mill workers by the mill owners also left a lot to be desired as the following descriptions from local doctors show:

(1) The house accommodation is generally bad, sometimes wretched... Sometimes a whole family inhabit a room, but there seems to be a good many females who are not living with their parents and are unmarried and board together... I frequently meet cases where the original tenant is a married man who, with his family, occupies the ground floor, all the other parts being sub-let.

(2) Very many females in this district sleep three or four in a bed in a small close apartment. The house accommodation in the neighbourhood of the mills is not fit to contain more than half the workers.

(3) (House Accommodation)— Not extra good in Falls district, sometimes from eight and nine persons sleep in one room.

(4) Since the Sanitary Act has come into force, house accommodation tolerable. The majority of the houses consist of kitchen, sleeping room and garret and the number of inhabitants about five and a fraction to each house.

And when it came to food:

(5) The poorest class... take tea again for their midday meal, which is reboiled at the dinner hour, and contains a quantity of Tannin, which confines the bowels very much.

(6) The diet principally used by the factory workers consists of tea and soda bread, occasionally a little broth with a large amount of vegetables. They are very dirty in their habits and extremely immoral.

Eventually, as a result of doctors' and inspectors' reports, improvements were made in the working conditions of the mill workers. In particular, better ventilation in the mills removed the danger from the 'pouce'. During the 20th century, the government and the city council have worked together to improve housing conditions. And, of course, doctors still complain about the way we eat in Northern Ireland!

SOURCE A is an advertisement for J. N. Richardson Sons & Owden Ltd., linen manufacturers of Belfast. Note not only the variety of linen products but also the worldwide addresses for the company. This shows the importance of the export market to the prosperity of the linen industry. Also note the awards won by the company at various trade fairs throughout the years.

PRONI D2826/64/8

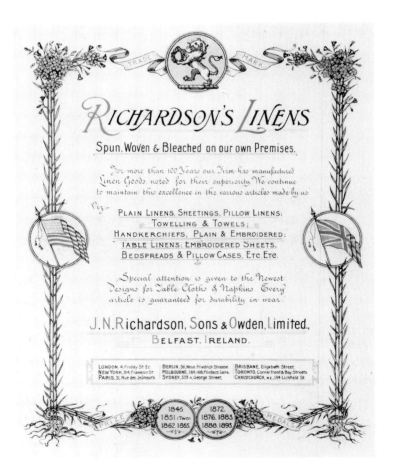

Index	Page
Washed Tea Cloth & Towels	1
Bleached	2
Loom Embroidery Cloth & Bleached Art Linen	2
Washed & Bleached Butchers Linen	3
Union Bleached Butchercloth & Bleached Tea Cloth	3
Loom & Bleached Sheetings	4
Bleached Pillow Linen	4
Glass Cloth Towels & Towelling	6
Glass Check Towels & Towelling & Glass Checked	7
Bird Eye & Pheasant Eye Diaper	9
Cloutings	10
Russia Diapers & Cloutings	11
Diaper Towels & Towelling	13/14
Loom & Bleached Damask Towelling	14
Brown Imperial & Crash Bath Towels	14
Crape Towels & Towelling	16
Washed Huck Towels & Towelling	18/19
Bleached	20
Devonshire Huck Towels & Towelling	19/21
Union Huck Towels	22

Index (Cont.ᵈ)	Page
Damask Huck Towels	23
Loom Damask Towels	25
Loom & Bleached S.H. Diaper & Damask Towels	27
Hemstitched & Spokestitched Towels	29/30
Loom Damask Napkins, Cloths & Pieces	32/33
Union Loom Damask Napkins, Cloths & Pieces	35
Creamed Damask Napkins, Cloths & Pieces	37/38
Bleached Damask Napkins, Cloths & Pieces	40/44
Fringed Bleached Damask Tray Cloths	44
Coloured Cotton Damask Covers & Tabling	46
" " Doylies	46
Rough Brown & Creamed Yarn Linens ⎫ See back of book	
Union Tea & Apron Cloth ⎭	
Sizes in inches of Bleached Damask	50/53
" " Tray Cloths	54

SOURCE B is the index from a linen traveller's pocket book. A linen traveller was the travelling salesman of the industry. This index shows the wide variety of material made from linen.
PRONI D 792/1.

SOURCE C are examples of the rather exotic labels used when exporting linen overseas. As you can see, they tried to capture the atmosphere of the countries to which linen was sent.
PRONI D1796/2.

REGULATIONS

WHICH MUST BE STRICTLY ATTENDED TO BY THE PERSONS EMPLOYED IN THE WORKS OF

JOHN AND WILLIAM CHARLEY & CO.

Persons employed in these works are to attend punctually, from day to day, to the established hours of the Concern.

Although the principal business of the Concern is executed by *piece-work*, the same attention to hours must be observed by those employed in that way, as by the workers paid per day.

If an individual employed on piece-work has executed all that may be ready for him to do at an early hour, he can, if circumstances permit, readily obtain permission to leave for the remainder of the day, either from the Manager, or the Overlooker of the department to which he belongs; but must not absent himself without such permission, under a penalty of One to Five Shillings.

All persons wishing to quit the employment must give a *fortnight's notice*,—the same notice will be given to every worker about to be parted with, should he not have forfeited his right to such by misconduct, or a breach of the regulations.

Workers giving a false account of the last place or places they have been employed at, or of the cause of their having left such place or places, may be discharged without warning.

Any person coming drunk to work, or behaving in a disorderly manner whilst upon the premises, or introducing spirituous liquors into the works, shall be subject to a fine of Ten Shillings for the first offence, and for the second, forfeit all wages due at the time, and be liable to be discharged without warning.

Workers shall be accountable for every article committed to their care, and will be charged for every damage done to them.

Persons employed here must not, on any pretence whatever, bring with them, or by any means introduce strangers into the works, without leave, under a penalty of Five Shillings.

Any person found in a workshop other than that in which he has business, shall forfeit Sixpence.

Any article lost out of the works must be accounted for, or paid for, by the persons to whose department it belonged; and every worker must be responsible for the breakage of windows opposite his own department.

The coats and trousers given to some of the workers are to be delivered up should the party leave the concern, or be dismissed, within one year from the time of his receiving such.

Every person employed here must execute the work entrusted to him carefully and correctly, and pass the goods through his department free of *careless or imperfect handling*, under a penalty to be regulated by the loss resulting from such carelessness.

Persons walking over goods on the field or grass, or dirtying or abusing them in any way, shall be subject to a fine from Sixpence upwards.

Any person committing nuisance, or leaving unseemly filth in any part of the premises, shall be subject to a fine of Sixpence upwards.

Any act of *mischief*, in any form, shall be punished by fine or dismissal.

Every person absenting himself without leave shall forfeit from One to Five Shillings.

No *smoking* allowed about any part of the works, except in the workers' fire-house, at meal hours.—Penalty for breach of this rule, Sixpence upwards.

No part of the property of the Concern, however trifling, to be carried off the premises without leave.

No washing permitted by any of the workers, except such articles as may belong to his own person.

No beetling of clothes allowed to any person whatever; and no one will be allowed to enter the engine-rooms but the loft-men and the persons employed therein.

Every piece of linen, or other material for bleaching, must be entered in the Office Books, and settled for when finished. Any pieces not entered, and concealed by any worker, will be liable to double the usual charge for bleaching.

Seymour Hill and **Mossvale** Bleachworks, 1st January, 1851.

SOURCE D is a copy of a notice of rules which had to be kept by the workforce at John and William Charley and Co., bleachers from Seymour Hill and Mossvale. These rules are typical of the regulations drawn up by employers in the middle of the 19th century.
PRONI D2242/7/19.

Learning activities

Q12　Look carefully at Source A and Source B.

(a)　Make a list of all the different types of goods which could be made from linen.

(b)　Write down the 10 cities where Richardson's Linens had offices.

(c)　Find out which countries these cities are in. How many continents are they in?

(d)　Which two flags are shown in Source A?

(e)　Why do you think Richardson's would show these two flags on their advertisements?

(f)　What sort of plant is shown growing in Source A?

(g)　Try to find out the meanings of the words DAMASK, DIAPER and HUCK as used in Source B.

Q13　Look carefully at Source C.

Either　(a)　Copy one of these labels into your workbook

or

(b)　Design your own label to place on linen being exported to either China or Australia.

Q14　Look carefully at Source D.

(a)　Make a list of all the reasons for which a worker could be fined.

(b)　What was the largest fine?

(c)　What was the smallest fine?

(d)　Look back to the wages in 1855. Would these fines have been a lot out of a worker's wages? To help you, note that sixpence = 2 $\frac{1}{2}$ p. and one shilling = 5p.

(e)　Do you think these rules were fair? Explain your answer as fully as you can.

Q15　How useful are Sources A, B and C to an historian studying the spread of the Belfast linen industry around the world?

Q16　How reliable is Source D to an historian studying the working conditions in linen mills? Can you think of what it does not tell you about life in a mill?

PORT AND HARBOUR

By the end of the 18th century, Belfast had a number of natural advantages which encouraged its development as a port.

1 Belfast Lough had a deep and wide entrance which gave easy access to ships under sail.

2 The Pool of Garmoyle provided a safe anchorage for ships.

3 Belfast was ideally placed to handle the increasing trade of the Lagan Valley.

Difficulties with the lough

However, there was one major problem which held back the growth of Belfast as a port. This was the mud and sand which was deposited at the head of Belfast Lough by the four rivers which meet at Belfast — the Lagan, the Farset, the Blackstaff and the Connswater.

Great mud flats and sandbanks clogged up the Lagan and allowed only small ships to sail up the river to dock at Belfast harbour, which was at this time at the end of High Street. Even these small ships could only enter and leave the port at high tide when sea water would raise the level of the river enough to allow the ships to float.

High Street, Belfast in 1831. Belfast Harbour is on the left of the picture.
Ulster Museum IC/High St/831.

Larger ships had to anchor in the Pool of Garmoyle and unload their cargoes on to these smaller ships, which were called lighters. This was a dangerous and expensive operation.

The influence of businessmen

The businessmen of Belfast realised that if their trade was to develop, improvements would have to be made to allow larger vessels to sail up the Lagan and reach the harbour.

In 1785, therefore, the Belfast Chamber of Commerce, which consisted of the leading businessmen and traders of the town, asked the Irish House of Commons in Dublin for £2000 in order to cut a deep water channel through the mud and sandbanks down to the Pool of Garmoyle.

The Irish Parliament refused to give the businessmen the money. However, they did say that responsibility for the control of the harbour should be removed from the Town Council and given to the businessmen of the town.

This meant that control of the development of the harbour was now in the hands of those men who were most interested in making Belfast a successful port.

The businessmen formed an organisation called 'The Corporation for preserving and improving the Port of Belfast'. Of course this title was too much of a mouthful and the organisation was more commonly called the Ballast Board. After 1847, the name was changed again to the Belfast Harbour Commissioners.

The growth of the port

By 1795, the Ballast Board had built the first dry dock in Belfast. This new dock was capable of holding up to 3 vessels of 200 tons at any one time. Individual businessmen also began to build their own quays. As a result of these improvements business in the port increased, as these figures show:

    1786 — 772 ships in port - total tonnage 34,287
    1813 — 1,190 ships in port - total tonnage 97,670

The development in 1830 of steam-powered dredgers meant that it would now be possible to make deep cuts through the mud and sandbanks to the Pool of Garmoyle. This would allow the largest ships to sail directly into Belfast harbour. Plans were drawn and work was begun.

The first cut was completed in 1841 by William Dargan. This made a channel with a minimum depth of 9 feet — enough clearance for most of the ships of that day. The mud and sand which was dredged up was dumped to form an island, at first called Dargan's Island and later Queen's Island.

Improvements continued throughout the 1840s. In 1845, the Ballast Board bought up all the privately owned quays. Now all of Belfast harbour was under one management and this would make further improvements much easier.

In 1849, a second cut was made and the Victoria Channel was opened. The opening of this channel prompted scenes of great celebration.

To hold the large vessels which could now reach Belfast, it was necessary to build a new quay. The new quay was called Donegall Quay and it completely replaced the old quays which were demolished and covered over to form Victoria Square, Albert Square and Corporation Square.

The docks were improved again in the 1860s. In 1889, the Alexandra Dock was opened. In 1899, the Musgrave Channel was opened.

By 1912, the amount of goods handled annually by Belfast docks passed the 3,000,000 ton mark. Due to the enterprise and persistence of Belfast businessmen, Belfast had become the third largest port in Great Britain, surpassed only by London and Liverpool. The transformation of Belfast's port and harbour was complete.

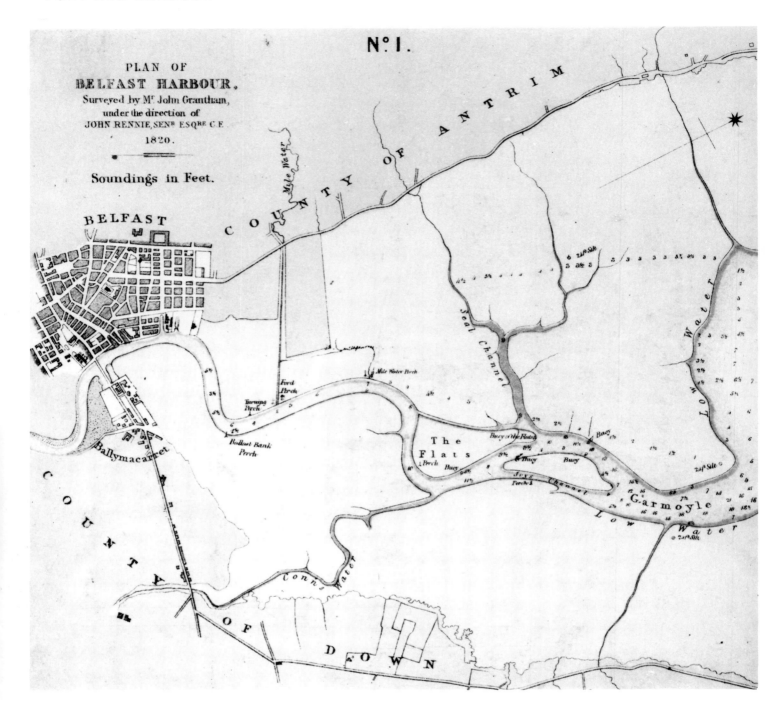

MAP A shows Belfast Harbour in 1820. The numbers in the water show the depth of the water in feet.
PRONI D2966/55.

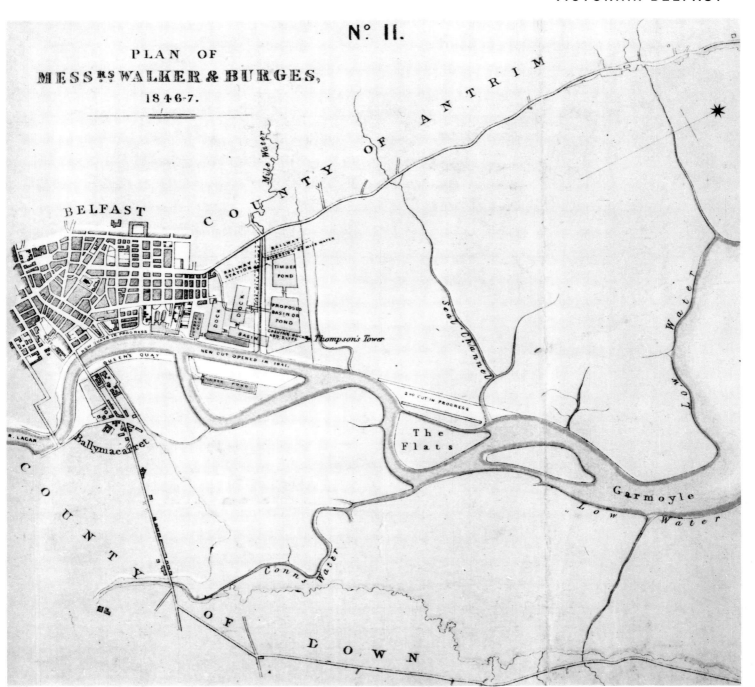

MAP B shows Belfast
Harbour in 1847.
Dargan's cut of 1841 is
clearly marked while the
second cut in progress
would form the Victoria
Channel opened in 1849.
PRONI D2966/55.

Learning activities

Q1 (a) In your workbooks, write the heading: *THE DEVELOPMENT OF BELFAST HARBOUR.*

(b) Now write one sentence describing events in each of these years which helped in the development of Belfast Harbour: 1785; 1795; 1830; 1841; 1845; 1849; 1889; 1899.

Q2 Copy this simple map of Belfast Harbour in 1820 into your workbooks. As you can see, it is based on MAP A on the previous page.

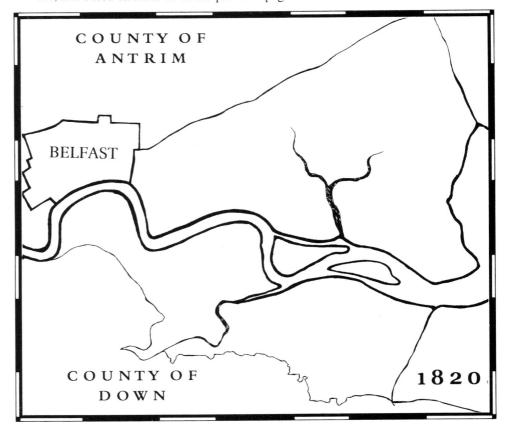

(a) Colour and label the River Lagan, the mud flats and the town of Belfast. Remember to use different colours and to work very neatly.

(b) Label the Pool of Garmoyle.

(c) Write two or three sentences describing the problems which would be faced by ships approaching Belfast Harbour in 1820.

Now look at MAP B which shows Belfast Harbour in 1847.

Can you spot the improvements which have been made?

(d) Carefully mark these improvements on the map in your workbook. Label each improvement.

(e) Which invention had to be developed before it became possible to make these improvements?

Q3 Which of the following factors of change were most important in encouraging the growth of the port of Belfast:

(a) The wish to make more money.

(b) The invention of machinery to deepen the lough.

(c) The needs of the linen industry.

Pick the factor which you think is most important and give as many reasons as possible for your answer.

Q4 Why do you think it was important to give businessmen control of the port rather than leave control of the port to the local council?

SHIPBUILDING

The early years

During the first half of the 19th century, shipbuilding in Belfast faced several serious problems.

1 The shallow water, mud and sandbanks of Belfast Lough, which held back the growth of the port, also held back the development of shipbuilding.

2 The wood used to build ships had to be imported as all of the accessible local timber had been cut down.

3 Belfast had no local supplies of iron or coal and this compared badly with shipyards at Glasgow or in England where iron and coal supplies were close at hand.

As a result, the early shipbuilding firms in Belfast — Ritchie & MacLaine, Charles Connell & Sons and Thompson & Kirwan — had only moderate success, building some 50 ships between 1820 and 1850.

Ritchie's Dock in 1810.
Ulster Museum
1E/2A/Ritchie/810.

Influence of the Harbour Commissioners

The improvements to the port in the 1840s solved the problem of the shallow water and allowed the Harbour Commissioners to reorganise not only the port of Belfast but also shipbuilding. The Harbour Commissioners wanted to keep the Co. Antrim side of the Lagan for docks and quays only. Shipbuilding was to be encouraged on the Co. Down side of the river and, in particular, on the newly formed Queen's Island.

Therefore, when Donegall Quay and the new Harbour Office were built on the site of the old shipyards, the Commissioners laid out a number of small shipyards on Queen's Island to encourage the development of the industry.

How Harland & Wolff began

In 1853, Robert Hickson, owner of a small ironworks in Eliza Street, took over one of the yards on Queen's Island to build iron ships. Hickson himself had limited knowledge of shipbuilding but he was fortunate in his choice of manager, a 23 year-old Yorkshireman who had learned the shipbuilding trade on the Clyde and the Tyne.

The young manager was called Edward Harland.

In the first four years, the yard produced two iron steamships, four iron sailing ships and a paddle-steamer. Then, in 1858, Harland, obviously eager to be his own boss, bought the yards from Hickson for £5,000. He was loaned the money by a friend of the family who lived in Liverpool called G. C. Schwabe. Schwabe's nephew at that time was personal assistant to Harland. His name was Gustave Wolff. Wolff became a full partner in the firm in 1861 and the firm became known as Harland and Wolff.

HARLAND AND WOLFF

How Harland & Wolff succeeded

The firm of Harland and Wolff was to grow into one of the largest shipbuilding firms in the world by the end of the century. The success of the company was all the more remarkable when we remember the problems faced by any shipbuilder based in Belfast. The problem of shallow water may have been solved but Belfast never acquired an iron or steel works to supply the shipyard and coal also had to be imported.

However, a number of factors ensured that Harland and Wolff would succeed where others had failed.

1 Shipping lines were demanding more and more ships from the 1860s onwards as, firstly, world trade and, later, emigration from Europe to the U.S.A. and other countries reached new heights.

2 One of the greatest problems for any new firm is to win orders in the face of competition from more experienced competitors. Gustave Wolff was able to win orders for the new firm because of his family connections with Liverpool shipping lines.

3 Having won the orders for ships, Harland was able to prove his technical genius for designing and building iron ships. As a result, the firm was able to establish a reputation for excellence and attracted more and more orders.

Family connections and inventions

Eighteen of the first twenty-five ocean-going ships built by Harland and Wolff were for the Bibby Line of Liverpool. G. C. Schwabe, Wolff's uncle and Harland's benefactor, was a partner in this company. This is a prime example of how family ties helped Harland and Wolff in their early years.

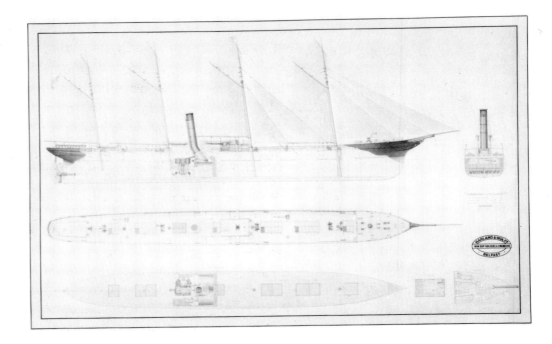

Plan of the *Grecian and Italian*, an example of a 'Bibby Coffin'.
Linenhall Library.

The three ships built for the Bibby Line in 1867 — the *Istrian, Iberian* and *Illyrian* — caused a sensation in the shipping world due to Harland's revolutionary design. The ships were long, narrow and had a flat bottom. Indeed, they were called 'Bibby Coffins' by their critics because of their box shape and because the critics believed they would not survive an ocean crossing.

Harland, however, had ensured the strength of the vessels by fitting iron decks, while the flat 'Belfast Bottom' ensured stability. As a result, the ships had not only a greater cargo-carrying capacity than their rivals but also had a greater speed. The insult of 'Bibby Coffins' was soon replaced by the admiring description of the ships as 'Ocean Greyhounds'.

The White Star Line

In 1870, a contract was signed with the Oceanic Steam Navigation Company of Liverpool, better known as the White Star Line. The contract was to build large passenger liners for the greatly increasing Atlantic trade.

The first White Star liner, the *Oceanic,* was launched in 1871 and it can be regarded as the first modern liner. Accommodation was placed for the first time across the full width of the ship and, on Harland's insistence, the first class accommodation was placed in the middle of the ship, away from the roll and vibration of the engines at the rear.

As a result, the *Oceanic* provided plentiful and cheap accommodation for emigrants to the USA while at the same time setting new standards in luxury for first class passengers. Indeed, the first class accommodation was described as being 'as comfortable as a Swiss hotel'.

The partnership with the White Star line guaranteed the future success of Harland and Wolff. The workforce of 500 in 1861 had increased to 2,400 by 1870. In 1880, Harland and Wolff set up their own works to build engines for the ships. In 1882, more slipways were added.

Bigger and better

The launch of the liners the *Teutonic* and the *Majestic* in 1889 introduced yet another innovation in ship design. These were twin-screw ships, which had two propellers and therefore a lot more power. As a result, the ships were bigger and faster than their rivals and, as if to prove the point, the *Teutonic* crossed the Atlantic in the record time of 6 days, 17 hours and 25 minutes on its maiden voyage.

This innovation prompted yet another expansion in shipbuilding at the yard. Output at Harland and Wolff rose from an average of 1,000 tons in 1880 to over 100,000 tons in the 1890s. By 1900, Harland and Wolff employed 9,000 men.

The success of Harland and Wolff prompted other firms to try their luck at shipbuilding. One of the most successful of the rival yards was Workman, Clark & Company, known as the 'wee yard'. McIlwaine & Coll also set up a yard on the Queen's Island, building smaller ships of up to 5,000 tons in size.

Learning activities

Q1 (a) Write two or three sentences describing the problems faced by shipbuilders in Belfast.

(b) Explain how each of these problems were overcome.

Q2 Divide into groups of four.

We want to find out why Harland and Wolff succeeded at shipbuilding in Belfast despite the problems which you have just written about.

(a) In your groups try to find as many reasons as you can to explain why Harland and Wolff succeeded. Make a list of these reasons (as you think of them).

(b) Select a spokesperson for your group. The spokesperson will now report back to the rest of the class. Try to spot if other groups have picked the same reasons for Harland and Wolff's success as your group. Make a list of the most popular reasons for success on the blackboard.

(c) Now go back into your groups and try to decide if shipbuilding would have succeeded in Belfast without Edward Harland and his partner Gustave Wolff. Would a change of managers have made a difference or not? Work out what your group thinks and write down any reasons for your answers. Compare your findings with other groups.

Q3 (a) The chapter describes three major improvements to ship design made by Edward Harland. Write a sentence describing each improvement.

(b) Explain how each improvement contributed to the success of Harland and Wolff.

Q4 Draw an example of a 'Bibby coffin'.

RULES

To be observed in these Works and subject to which all persons employed are engaged.

1. Ordinary working hours from 6.20 till 8.20 o'clock; from 9 till 1 o'clock; and from 2 till 5.30 o'clock. On Saturdays work will cease at 1.30 o'clock, but without interval for dinner. Wages will be paid by the hour; and only the number of hours actually worked will be paid for. Any workman commencing work and absenting himself without leave until the termination of the ordinary working day, will not be entitled to payment for any time he may have worked on the day in question.

2. The first two hours of Overtime, Saturdays included, to be paid for as time and a quarter, and further Overtime to count as time and a half; but no time will be counted as Overtime until the ordinary number of hours for the day has been completed. Sunday work, when absolutely necessary, will be paid for as double ordinary time.

3. Workmen on the night shift to start work at 5.30 p.m., and continue until 6.20 o'clock the next morning; intervals for meals from 9 till 9.25 p.m., and 1.35 till 2 o'clock a.m. For the hours worked on the night shift, time and a quarter will be paid.

4. Wages will be paid fortnightly on each alternate Saturday, at 1.30 o'clock—to be counted up to the previous Thursday night, and from it the amount of any fines, debts, or damages will be deducted. Men off work on the pay day will not be paid until after those working have received their wages.

5. All hands will enter the Works through the Time Offices at starting time, and also on resuming work after breakfast and dinner. Each workman to draw his Time Board on commencing work; and on resuming work after breakfast and dinner, must, as he enters the Works, take his Token off the Board and put it into the receiving slot. On leaving work each workman to pass out through the Time Offices and hand in his Time Board, with the amount of time worked and for what purpose written thereon, and on each Thursday evening the total amount of the previous week's time to be written thereon. Any breach of this Rule will subject him to a fine, and any workman not delivering his Token or Time Board personally at the times mentioned will forfeit all claim to wages for that day. All workmen passing through the gates during working hours must show their Time Boards to the Gatekeeper and give any explanation that may be demanded as to their business; non-compliance with this will forfeit wages for the day and subject the offender to fine or dismissal.

6. Those provided with Tool Boxes or Lockers to leave the keys thereof at the Office or Store before quitting work, if so ordered.

7. Any one causing disturbance in the Works, neglecting the orders of his Foreman, avoidably absent for more than one day without the leave of his Foreman, bringing spirituous liquors into the Works, or appearing here in a state of intoxication, will be subject to fine or dismissal.

8. Any one carelessly or maliciously breaking, injuring, or defacing any Machine or Tool, altering any Template, removing Shores without leave, or committing any other mischief, to pay the cost of repairing the same, or, in the option of the Employers, to be fined.

9. Those provided with Tools must satisfactorily account for the same before leaving the employment, or the value of any that may be missing will be deducted from the wages due.

10. Any one entering or leaving the Works except by the appointed gates, or carrying out material to ships without having it charged by the Storekeeper and also giving account of same to the Gateman, will be subject to fine or dismissal.

11. No person is allowed to take strangers into any portion of the Works without first having obtained an authorized pass.

12. Any one stopping work, or preparing to stop work before the appointed time, will be fined or dismissed.

13. Any one wasting, injuring, or destroying Oil, Pitch, Tar, Oakum, Paint, Candles, Nails, or any other material, to pay the cost thereof.

14. Any one smoking, or preparing food during working hours, or smoking at any other time near combustile material, will be fined or dismissed.

15. Any one leaving a candle, lamp, or fire burning after use, will be fined.

16. In the event of work being spoiled by the carelessness of workmen, the labour expended thereon will not be paid for, and those in fault will be held responsible for the loss of the material.

We reserve to ourselves the right of fining for any irregularity or offence not specially mentioned in the foregoing Rules.

HARLAND & WOLFF.

Shipbuilding and Engineering Works,
Belfast, 30th May, 1888.

SOURCE A shows the rules of work at Harland and Wolff in 1888.
PRONI D2910.

SOURCE B shows an extract from a wages book at Harland and Wolff in 1888.
PRONI D2805/WB/2/1.

This Indenture, MADE the _Fourth_ day of _March_ in the year of our Lord One Thousand Eight Hundred and Seventy _two_ between EDWARD JAMES HARLAND and GUSTAVUS WILLIAM WOLFF, of Queen's Island, in the County of Down, Iron Shipbuilders and Engineers, trading under the Firm of HARLAND & WOLFF, of the one part, and _John Carr the younger_ of _Ballymacarret_ in the County of _Down_ of the other part, **Witnesseth,** that the said _John Carr by and with the consent and approval of his father John Carr Mariner of Ballymacarret in the county of Down as testified by his signing hereof_ doth put himself APPRENTICE to the said EDWARD JAMES HARLAND and GUSTAVUS WILLIAM WOLFF to learn the Art and Trade of _a Millwright_ and with them, after the manner of an Apprentice, to serve for and during the full term and space of _Five_ years, to be computed from the _First_ day of _January_ One Thousand Eight Hundred and Seventy _two_ to be fully complete and ended. During which term the said Apprentice his said Masters faithfully shall serve, their secrets keep, their lawful commands everywhere gladly do ; he shall do no damage to his said Masters in their goods, chattels, or estate, or know or procure any to be done by others ; but when he shall know, or have any reason to suspect any such being intended, he shall forthwith give warning to his said Masters of the same ; he shall not waste the goods of his said Masters, or give or lend them unlawfully to any ; he shall not commit fornication, or contract matrimony within the said term ; hurt, to said Masters in their persons or families, he shall not do, cause, or procure to be done by others ; he shall not play cards, dice, or any unlawful game with his own or others' goods, whereby his said Masters may have loss, during the said term. Without license of his said Masters he shall neither buy nor sell ; he shall not frequent taverns, alehouses, or playhouses, or absent himself from his said Masters' service day or night unlawfully, under the forfeiture of one week's wages for each day he absents himself, or serving two days for one at the expiry of his said apprenticeship, at the option of his said Masters, but in all things, as an honest and faithful Apprentice, he shall behave himself towards his said Masters and their managers, during the said term. AND the said Masters said Apprentice the aforesaid art which they use, by the best way and means that they can, shall teach, instruct, or cause to be instructed in, with due correction ; and unto their said Apprentice shall pay in consideration of his service

During the first year	_Six Shillings per week_
During the Second year	_Seven Shillings per week_
During the third year	_Eight Shillings per week_
During the fourth year	_Nine Shillings per week_
During the fifth year	_Ten Shillings per week_

In Witness whereof, the parties above named have hereunto respectively set their hands and seals, the day and year aforesaid.

Signed, Sealed, and Delivered
in the presence of

John Kerr
John Kerr
E J Harland
G W Wolff

William McGarry
Robert Macnaughton

SOURCE C shows part of an apprenticeship indenture at Harland and Wolff, dated 1872.
PRONI D3540/1.

Learning activities

Q5 Look carefully at Source A.

(a) How many hours each day were you expected to work?

(b) How many hours a week were you expected to work?

(c) How many hours a day did you work if you were on the night-shift?

(d) Did you receive extra pay for working at night?

(e) Why would the firm want people to work at night?

(f) How did the firm know how many hours each person had worked that week?

(g) Why could a worker be fined? Note down all the reasons in your own words.

Q6 Look carefully at Source B. Remember that these wages are for two weeks' work.

(a) How much did each man get paid per week?

(b) How do these wages compare to wages in the linen industry?
(see chapter on linen).

(c) Why do you think the wages were so much better in shipbuilding?

Q7 Look carefully at Source C.

(a) What is an apprentice?

(b) How long did John Carr have to serve as an apprentice at Harland and Wolff?

(c) What trade was John Carr learning?

(d) How much did he get paid while he was an apprentice?

(e) How do these wages compare with wages in the linen industry?
(see chapter on linen).

Q8 Compare the rules for Harland and Wolff (Source A) with the rules for Charley's linen mill on page.

(a) list any similarities

(b) list any differences

(c) Would you rather have worked in a linen mill or the shipyard under these rules? Explain your answer.

Q9 These sources provide information about rules and conditions of work, wages and apprenticeships in the Belfast shipyards. If an historian wanted to make a comparison between working conditions in the linen industry and the shipbuilding industry in the late 19th century, what other sources of information would he find useful?

OTHER INDUSTRIES

The continuing growth and prosperity of Belfast in the late 19th century rested not only on the linen and shipbuilding industries but on a wide range of economic activity.

Indeed, a book published in 1891, called *The Industries of Ireland*, listed over 300 firms of various sizes in the city of Belfast.

Engineering

This chapter will not attempt to describe what each of those firms produced but rather to give some idea of the wide variety of goods produced in Belfast towards the end of the 19th century.

Belfast was never able to establish a profitable iron and steel industry as it did not have access to the cheap coal and iron ore available to iron foundries in England and Scotland. Even Harland and Wolff and Workman, Clark and Co. found it more profitable to have their own foundries on the Clyde in Scotland and transport the finished iron and steel sheets across to Belfast.

The struggling iron foundries of Belfast, therefore, began to specialise in the production of steam engines, boilers and machinery for factories both at home and abroad.

Examples of engineering firms in Belfast which established a worldwide reputation were:

(a) **The Falls Foundry.**

Established by James Combe in 1845 and later known as Combe Barbour. The firm specialised in textile machinery not only for the mills of Belfast but for mills around the world. For example, Combe Barbour built engines for cotton mills in India.

(b) **James Mackie and Sons.**

This firm was founded in 1852 and specialised in the production of textile machinery.

(c) **Musgrave Bros.**

This firm was established in 1855 and were makers of high quality stable and house fittings, counting most of the royal families of Europe among their customers.

(d) **Sirocco Works.**

Samuel Davidson established his 'Sirocco' works in Belfast specialising in the production of tea-drying equipment for use on Davidson's own tea estates in India. The firm later expanded its production to include all types of ventilation and fan manufacture.

Ropemaking

In the 1870s, Harland and Wolff required a large and reliable source of rope for their shipyard. Therefore, in 1873, Edward Harland helped to set up the Belfast Ropework Co. These ropeworks imported hemp from the Philippines, bathed them in oil and, as a result, produced the best quality rope available for shipping. In addition, the firm produced twine for the new reaping machines on the farms, string for window blinds and cord for fishing and trawler nets.

By 1900, the Belfast Ropework Co. had proved so successful that it could claim to be the largest single ropeworks in the world.

Belfast Ropeworks.
PRONI D2889/P/4/1.

Two large tobacco firms were established in Belfast by 1900.

Tobacco

(a) Murray's was founded in 1810 and moved into their Linfield Road factory in the 1890s. They still produce their world famous Erinmore pipe tobacco on these premises.

(b) Thomas Gallaher moved his tobacco business from Londonderry to Belfast in 1863. By 1900, Gallaher's was the largest tobacco factory in Ireland and employed over 1,600 people.

Food and drink

(a) Baking and flour milling became increasingly important activities during the century with the need to feed the ever-growing population of the town. Major firms were Bernard Hughes and Inglis and Co.

(b) There were four main whiskey distilleries in Belfast by the end of the century. The largest distillery was Dunville's on the Grosvenor Road which produced over 3 million gallons of whiskey and employed 500 people in 1900.

(c) The production of aerated water (what we would today call lemonade) was another large export industry for Belfast. Firms such as Ross's, Cantrell and Cochrane, Grattan's and Corry's used the water from artesian springs over 200 feet under Belfast and were able to sell their products throughout the Empire and particularly in areas where the drinking water was considered dangerous.

Printing

Belfast maintained its reputation as a centre for publishing and printing during the 19th century. The firm of Marcus Ward & Co. was particularly successful, not only producing books and illustrations of the highest quality but also popularising the Christmas card and the tear-off calendar.

Tyres

In 1887, John Boyd Dunlop, who had come to Belfast from Scotland in 1867 to practise as a vet, developed a pneumatic tyre for his son's tricycle. By 1890, he had opened a small business manufacturing these pneumatic tyres. This was to be the forerunner of today's massive Dunlop company.

Cars

The Chambers brothers produced cars in Belfast from 1904 until 1927 when cheaper mass-produced vehicles forced the firm to close.

Solve the clues and then find the answers in the wordsquare. All of the clues refer to industries in Belfast.

Clues

1 Water filled with bubbles — like lemonade. (7,5)
2 A Belfast printing firm. (6,4)
3 Tyre filled with air. (9)
4 _____ & Cochrane were famous for their water. (8)
5 Falls Foundry was also known as Combe _____. (7)
6 Industry concerned with making bread. (6)
7 A baker. (6)
8 These were made in Belfast by the Chambers brothers. (4)
9 This firm made stable and house fittings for royalty. (8,4)
10 He moved his tobacco firm from Londonderry to Belfast. (8)
11 Samuel _____ had tea estates in India. (8)
12 Famous for their aerated water. (7)
13 Smoked in pipes and latterly cigarettes. (7)
14 A vet who developed a tyre. (6)
15 Made in a bakery. (5)
16 This company was famed for its ginger ale. (4)
17 Industry concerned with making machines for other factories. (11)
18 The largest distillery in Belfast. (9)
19 They made cars in Belfast. (8)
20 A shipbuilder who wanted some rope! (7)
21 The name of this firm making tea-drying equipment is also a warm wind. (7)
22 Bernard _____ the baker! (6)
23 These go on the wheels of bicycles or cars. (5)
24 The process of making whiskey. (10)
25 A place were rope is made. (9)
26 Marcus Ward were successful at this. (8)
27 This product was made by Dunville's and other distillers. (7)
28 This firm specialised in the production of textile machinery. (7)
29 Firm famous for their Erinmore tobacco. (6)
30 Raw material used in making rope. (4)

Wordsquare

```
F S E H G U H P O L N U D P R K Q W C L
H T G G L P S R Z G N L L L E R T N A C
N S E D A V I D S O N Z F N A T T A R G
D V S E Y S I L G N I C D X Q E R Q C J
A X X L M K G Z D R D W K W S E R Y T Y
E I E P P M E H F K X T V T A Z P P A A
R F T S R A C Y G N F T J W Y A R R U M
B V P C Z J I C Z Y G N I L L I T S I D
V R E L T O B A C C O C J S K N X Q T N
P M X C K G Y K Y U E H G D D J G F S Z
B A E R A T E D W A T E R U I G X Y P U
G N I R E E N I G N E N X D N A L R A H
Q B G B G F D R A W S U C R A M X F R V
M M N R O P E W O R K S N G N I K A B E
A G I S I R O C C O B H G W H I S K E Y
C J T L D F C I T A M U E N P D T F F L
K F N Y U M U S G R A V E B R O S Q J U
I E I I E T S P B A R B O U R V S S O R
E S R E B M A H C G A L L A H E R M N F
S X P U E W O M A S E L L I V N U D C S
```

Q2 (a) Look back to the list of exports from Belfast at the end of the 17th century (p. 5). Now, using the information given in the last three chapters, make a list of exports from Belfast at the end of the 19th century.

(b) Can you think of reasons why the 2 lists are so different? Make a note of these reasons.

(c) Which are the most important reasons for the increase in the range of goods exported from Belfast?

TRANSPORT

Outside Belfast

During the 19th century, Belfast continued to serve as the market town for the farmers of the Lagan valley and surrounding countryside. The improvements in the port and harbour facilities in the early 19th century increased the importance of Belfast to this local area as a link with the markets of mainland Britain.

However, farmers in the rest of the province initially had difficulty in taking advantage of these improvements as it was so difficult to transport their goods to Belfast. This was because not many roads of good quality led to Belfast in the early 19th century. For example, the main road between Belfast and Antrim, which was Belfast's main link to the north of the province, was only built in the 1830s. Large areas of the countryside were left untouched by canals.

Railways

The introduction of the railway to the province completely changed this picture. Railways could carry linens and agricultural goods from all parts of the Ulster countryside to Belfast where they could be processed and shipped to mainland Britain and around the world.

In return, even remote areas of the province could enjoy imports of cotton and pottery from England and foodstuffs such as grain and bacon from America and tea, sugar and groceries from the Empire. As a result, the eating habits of the Ulster population changed from a diet of potatoes, oatmeal and dairy produce to one of much greater variety.

ULSTER RAILWAY.

THE PUBLIC are respectfully informed, that the First Section of this Line, from BELFAST to LIS-BURN, will be Opened, for the transit of PASSENGERS,

On MONDAY, the 12th of August.

HOURS OF STARTING :

From Belfast.	From Lisburn.
7, A.M.	8, A.M.
9, do.	10, do.
11, do.	12, Noon.
1, P.M.	2, P.M.
3, do.	4, do.
5, do.	6, do.
7, do.	8, do.

Each Train will stop at DUNMURRY, for One Minute, going and returning, to receive or set down Passengers.

Fares :

1st Class Carriage, 1s. each Passenger.
2nd Do.   Do.   6d.   Do.

No Reduction for the intermediate Stage.

Children......... Half Price.

JAMES GODDARD,
Chairman of Directors.

Belfast, 2d August, 1839.   (587

The first railway in Ulster was opened on the 12th August 1839 and ran between Belfast and Lisburn. Newspapers of the time carried the advertisements shown on the previous page informing the public of the new service.

The railway network

This line was extended to Lurgan and Portadown over the next few years and eventually was linked to the line from Dublin. At first, these lines were known as the Ulster Railway but, by 1875, the lines were taken over by the Great Northern Railway.

The Belfast and Northern Counties Railway operated lines to the north of Belfast while the north Down area was served by the Belfast and County Down Railway Company.

As the map shows, the lines spread out from Belfast enabling the city to reach all areas of the province and keep its position as the centre of trade and commerce in the North of Ireland.

Such progress was not welcomed by everyone, however. The practice of trains running on a Sunday, in particular, was frowned upon by one minister who declared:

'Every sound of a railway whistle is answered by a shout in hell.'

GNR Railway Station on
Gt Victoria St.
Ulster Museum, W10/29/19.

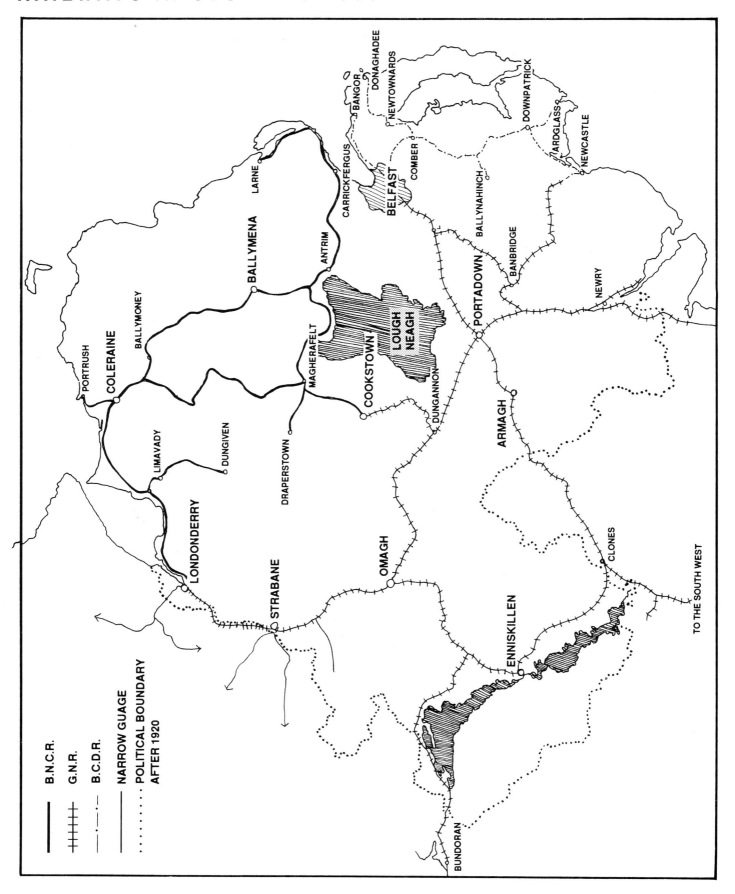

B.N.C.R.
G.N.R.
B.C.D.R.
NARROW GUAGE
POLITICAL BOUNDARY
AFTER 1920

Learning activities

1   Trace or copy the map showing the railways in Ulster in 1900. Start each line from Belfast and concentrate on one line at a time. Label your map 'Railways in Ulster c.1900'.

2   Write two or three sentences describing the benefits which the railways brought to towns such as Omagh or Strabane.

3   Write two or three sentences describing the benefits which the railways brought to Belfast.

4   Look carefully at the advertisement for the opening of the first railway line between Belfast and Lisburn and answer the questions which follow.

   (a) How many return journeys did the train make in one day?

   (b) Did the train make any stops? If so, where and for how long?

   (c) What were the fares for 1st class passengers, 2nd class passengers and children?

   (d) Do you think working class people could afford these fares? Look back to the chapter on linen to remind yourself of wages at the time.

5   (a) Why do you think the minister declared that 'Every sound of a railway whistle is answered by a shout in hell'?

   (b) Do you think other people in the community would have agreed with the minister? Note down the type of people who would agree and why they would agree. Note down the types of people who would not agree and why not.

6   Lines, such as the Belfast and Northern Counties Railway, were actually made up of lots of small railway companies, each with its own badge. Here are some examples. Copy some of these railway badges into your workbook. Colour the badges to make them bright and attractive.

INSIDE BELFAST

Horse-drawn carriages

Until the 1870s, public transport inside Belfast was for the wealthier classes only. Horse-drawn carriages charged up to 6d. a mile to carry passengers from the railway stations to hotels or to the new housing developments on the Malone ridge. Such prices were far beyond the reach of the ordinary working man.

An alternative was available. If carriages were pulled along on rails rather than on the road surface, there was a lot less friction. This meant that two horses could pull very large carriages containing many more people. As a result, much lower fares could be charged.

These carriages were called trams and were already operating successfully in the cities of mainland Britain. The only problem which delayed the introduction of trams to Belfast was the initial cost of laying the rails on the roads to support the trams.

Trams — transport for all

In 1872, a group of Belfast businessmen established the Belfast Street Tramways Company and began laying rails. The first line ran from Castle Place to Botanic Gardens. Poor management held back the development of the company in its early years and it was not until 1881, when Andrew Nance was appointed as general manager, that the trams began to challenge the horse-drawn carriages for customers.

Nance was to remain in charge until 1917 and under his management the whole face of public transport changed in Belfast to the benefit of everyone.

Firstly, Nance ordered the development of many more lines, spreading in all directions from Castle Junction in the centre of the city. Lines were built to Newtownbreda (1885), Malone Park (1888), Sydenham and Tennant Street (1889) and Ligonel (1892).

Also, in 1892, Nance introduced the new penny (1d.) fare. The horse-drawn carriages could not compete against such a wide variety of routes and such cheap fares and, in 1892, went out of business.

Horse drawn trams at Castle Junction.
Ulster Museum. W10/21/12.

The triumph of the tram service was now complete and the popularity of the trams grew rapidly with the public, as the following passenger figures show.

1881 — 1 million passengers
1891 — 10 million passengers
1904 — 28 million passengers

Most importantly, cheap and regular public transport allowed working class families to move away from the centre of town and houses built close to their place of work and, instead, look for better accommodation in more attractive areas of the city. This demand for new property was rapidly met by the builders of the period.

Learning activities

Q1 Write one sentence explaining the main difference between a horse-drawn carriage and a horse-drawn tram.

Q2 Write one sentence explaining how the development of trams helped encourage the growth of the city of Belfast.

Q3 Copy out the following paragraphs and fill in the gaps:

In 1872, the B_____ S_____ T_____ C_____ was formed. In 1881, A_____ N_____ was appointed general manager.

Nance ordered the development of tram lines to all parts of the city. Lines were built to N_____ in 1885, M_____ P_____ in 1888, S_____ and T_____ S_____ in 1889 and L_____ in 1892.

In 1892, Nance introduced a new fare of only o__ p_____. The horse-drawn carriages could not compete with such low fares and, in 1892, finally went out of business.

Q4 Draw a timeline showing changes in transport 1830-1900.

Q5 The following factors of change played a part in the development of transport in Belfast and Northern Ireland. Which factor do you think was most important? Give reasons for your answer.

(a) Economic.

(b) Invention.

(c) Individuals such as Nance.

HOUSING

Houses for the poor

We have already considered the poor housing conditions endured by the mill workers of Belfast in the chapter on linen. Their houses were built close to the factories by the mill owners and normally consisted of 4 rooms and 2 storeys. The rooms measured between 7 and 10 feet square and ceilings were 8 feet high downstairs and 6 feet high upstairs. It was quite common for 2 families to occupy these houses with between 18 and 20 people squeezing into the small rooms.

One observer at the time described the conditions in such a house:

> (In) Brady's Row... we found that 7 persons live and sleep in the same room — their beds, if such a thing they be called, lying upon the floor. The desolation and wretchedness of this apartment — without windows and open in all directions — it is utterly impossible to describe.

Learning activities

Q1   Look again at the size of rooms in the old mill houses.

Either: (a) Measure out an area 10 feet by 10 feet in your classroom.

or

(b) Find a room at home approximately 10 feet by 10 feet.

Now try to imagine between 8 and 10 people living and sleeping in that space. Where would they sleep? Where would they eat? Would it be clean or messy? Would it be stuffy? Would you have liked to live in such conditions?

Write down all your ideas. Compare your ideas with others in the class.

Why do you think people would be willing to live in such conditions?

Write down any ideas you might have in answer to this question.

Houses for the rich

The mill owners, on the other hand, used their profits to build great mansions on the outskirts of the town. Two examples are Glenburn House in Ballysillan and Strathern, built by H. A. M. Barbour who owned Hilden Mill outside Lisburn.

The middle and professional classes, during the first half of the century, lived in the centre of town around Donegall Place and College Square. The building of Queen's College, later to become Queen's University, encouraged the building of some houses at the bottom of the Malone ridge after 1850. However the rate at which houses were built remained slow at this time.

The housing boom

It was not until after 1870 that the great increase in the rate of house building in Belfast began. Between 1870 and 1900, the number of houses in Belfast increased four times over. Builders, such as H. & J. Martin, and estate agents, such as R. J. McConnell, built houses confident that they would find families to buy or rent the property.

Two main factors combined to produce this great boom in housing development in Belfast during this period.

1 People had more money. The increase in the number of skilled jobs in the shipbuilding and engineering industries meant that wages were higher. Therefore working class families could afford to rent better quality accommodation.

2 People did not have to live close to their place of work anymore. With trams providing cheap public transport, it was possible to move away from the dirty, crowded conditions in the centre of town and live in the newly developing suburban areas of Belfast.

The introduction of building regulations ensured that houses built during this period were a vast improvement on the earlier mill houses. Look carefully at the two photographs labelled Picture A and Picture B.

Picture A

Raphael Street.
Ulster Museum. W10/29/42.

Picture B

Rear view of houses in Smithfield area.
Ulster Museum. W10/21/250.

Picture A shows Raphael Street. Note the following features:

(a) Shutters on the downstairs windows for privacy and heat insulation.

(b) Footscrapers set into the wall by the front door to get rid of street dirt before entering the house.

(c) A footpath.

(d) A manhole, which tells us that there must have been drains and a water supply.

(e) A streetlight.

Picture B shows a rear view of houses in the Smithfield area. In this photograph the features to note are:

(a) A yard at least 10 feet square, each with its own privy.

(b) An entry at the back to allow for the disposal of rubbish and the emptying of the earth privies.

Learning activities

Q2 (a) Write a heading *IMPROVEMENTS TO WORKING CLASS HOUSING*.

(b) Make a list of all the improvements shown in these photographs.

(c) Write a sentence on each improvement explaining how this would make life more comfortable for people living in these houses.

Q3 Write down TWO reasons why people were able to move into this better quality accommodation.

Q4 How useful are the photographs in the text to the historian studying changes in housing in Belfast in the 19th century?

Q5 Are photographs always reliable as evidence for the historian?
Think carefully and give reasons for your answer.

How others saw Belfast Housing

It is worth noting that immigrants from Glasgow were amazed at the good quality of housing and the low rents in Belfast. This is probably because Belfast began its growth later than cities such as Glasgow and Manchester and therefore, because building regulations had already been passed, avoided some of the very worst housing conditions experienced in those cities.

It was during these final years of the century that the suburbs of Belfast along the Antrim, Woodvale, Ormeau and Ravenhill roads were built. Grander houses and developments such as Malone and Rosetta were also built at this time.

The frantic building activity of the time was described by the Ulster artist, Paul Henry, in the 1880s, in this manner:

From the Botanic Gardens and up the Malone Road, the roads were kept clean by clumsy contrivances known as scrapers: the mud which had been allowed to accumulate was put into carts and taken off to any depression in the fields and there dumped to form the groundwork and foundations for new houses which were springing up everwhere. For Belfast was growing up.... There were very large deposits of the red loam from which bricks are made in the neighbourhood of Belfast, and there were limestone quarries of considerable extent on the Cave Hill. In my childhood there was no more familiar sight than the unending procession of carts of bricks with which Belfast was feverishly built....

Learning activities

Q4 Copy the grid into your workbook and solve the clues. All of the answers are in this chapter. When all the answers have been filled in you should find the KEY WORD, which is something found on the Cave Hill.

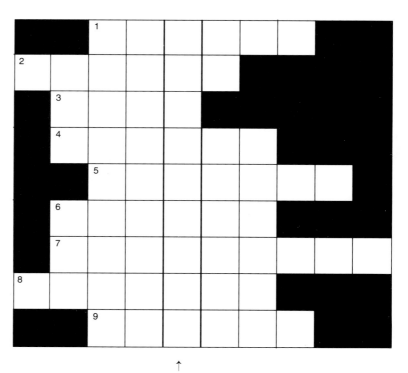

KEY

WORD

Clues

1. Some grand houses built here after 1850.
2. H. & J._____, the builder.
3. Red material, used in making bricks.
4. Suburban area in South Belfast.
5. Very grand housing development in South Belfast.
6. Most of the new houses were not bought, but _____.
7. R. J. _____ were well-known estate agents of the time.
8. These gardens are at the bottom of the Malone Road.
9. The building of this college encouraged some housing development.

ENTERTAINMENT AND LEISURE

'Pleasure in Belfast is a very secondary consideration'

This statement, made by a visitor to Belfast in the 19th century, creates the impression that Belfast, during Victorian times, must have seemed concerned with business, commerce and little else.

In part, this impression was true and, as we shall see, when the choice lay between business and pleasure, business always came first. However, when opportunities for entertainment and leisure did arise, they were eagerly accepted by the town's population.

(1)   Public holidays provided an excuse to escape into the countryside. At the beginning of the 19th century, a favourite spot for such an outing, particularly on Easter Monday, was the Cave Hill. People would bring picnics, listen to bands and enjoy rolling their eggs down the hill.

(2)   The Botanical Gardens were normally closed to the general public but were opened on occasional days when various activities would be organised for public amusement. For instance, in 1839 a fête was organised in the Botanical Gardens at which there was archery, tight-rope walking, conjuring, balloons, children's games, an exhibition of flowers and displays of camera obscura and the magic lantern.

Botanic Gardens, Belfast
c.1890.
Ulster Museum W10/79/3.

(3)   When the Queen's Island was formed following improvements to the port and harbour, it was decided to turn part of the island into a public park. The park was designed with a broad path, set at regular intervals with iron benches. A wire fence enclosed grass plots and flower beds and, in the middle of the island, a large glass house growing more exotic plants was built. Belfast's first zoo was also set on Queen's Island with monkeys, raccoons and birds such as parrots and a golden eagle.

The island proved to be very popular with the working classes between 1850 and 1870. However, once the shipyards needed to expand, Harland and Wolff took over the park with very little argument.

(4)   Towards the end of the century, further public parks were provided for the population of the town. With the growth of cheap public transport, it became much easier to enjoy a Sunday afternoon in parks at Ormeau, Woodvale, Alexandra, Falls or Victoria.

(5)   The development of the railway in the latter part of the century also opened new leisure opportunities for the population of Belfast who could travel to the seaside at Bangor or Whitehead or further afield to Portrush or Newcastle.

Great Victoria Railway
Station c.1910.
Ulster Museum W/10/46/13.

(6)   The railway also allowed people from outside Belfast to come into the city more easily to enjoy shows at the theatre. Theatres in Belfast had been frowned upon during the early part of the century as the audiences were often guilty of rowdy and drunken behaviour. However, by the 1870s, theatres such as the Theatre Royal were attracting players from around Britain to perform in tearful melodramas or musical entertainments.

The opening of the Grand Opera House in 1895 clearly demonstrated that theatre-going had once again become a respectable activity and many popular entertainments including circuses and pantomime were presented in the new theatre.

Learning activities

Q1   Find one example in this chapter which seems to prove the visitor's statement that in Belfast pleasure always came second to business.

Q2   Find three examples which show how improvements in transport helped improve leisure time.

Q3   Why do you think public parks were so popular with the people of Belfast? Remember what you have learned about housing and working conditions as you think about your answer.

Q4   Either:

   (a) Imagine attending the fête in the Botanical Gardens in 1839. You are with your mother, father and two brothers. Describe your excitement at getting into the gardens for the first time, the different activities taking place in the park and your return home.

                                   or

   (b) Imagine a visit to Queen's Island in 1865. Describe your walk around the park and a visit to the zoo. Describe not only what you see but also how pleased you are to escape the dirty, cramped streets of the town for an afternoon.

Painting of a riot at Boyne
Bridge.
Ulster Museum 1F/857/Riot.

Riot in 1846.
Ulster Museum 1F/804/Riot.

COMMUNITY RELATIONS IN BELFAST DURING THE 19TH CENTURY

Relations between the Protestant and Roman Catholic communities in Belfast could not have been better at the end of the 18th century.

In 1784, the first Roman Catholic chapel built in Belfast was opened in Chapel Lane. The building of the chapel had been largely paid for by the Protestants of the town and the opening, as reported in the *News Letter*, was an occasion for celebration:

> *On Sunday last, the Belfast First Co. and the Belfast Volunteer Co. paraded in full dress and marched to mass where a sermon was preached by the Rev. Mr. O'Donnell and a handsome collection made to aid in defraying the expense of erecting the new mass house. Great numbers of other protestant inhabitants also attended.*

In 1793, as delegates of the Catholic Convention passed through Belfast on their way to London to press their claims for political rights, the townspeople turned out to cheer them on their way.

As late as 1815, when the second Roman Catholic chapel was opened in Belfast in Donegall Street, the Catholics of Belfast published a note in the newspapers of the day thanking '*our much esteemed Protestant and Dissenting Brethren of Belfast*' for their generosity in helping build the chapel.

By the late 1820s, however, the Catholic Bishop of Down and Connor had to warn his parishioners to stay away from the festivities on the Cave Hill on Easter Monday for fear of trouble due to an Orange demonstration.

The election of 1832 saw riots on the streets of Belfast between Catholic and Protestant mobs and, after the election of 1835, the *News Letter* reported how a crowd:

> *on their way home smashed the windows of almost every Roman Catholic whose house they passed and the windows of not a few Protestants whose political sentiments were supposed to differ from theirs, while another mob attacked the homes of some Orangemen.*

The table below records only some of the riots which where to become a feature of life in Belfast throughout the 19th century:

DATE RIOT BEGAN	DURATION OF RIOT	DEATHS OR INJURIES
12 July 1832	1 day	4 deaths
12 July 1852	5-7 days	1 death
12 July 1857	56 days	Indefinite number injured
8 August 1864	18 days	12 deaths; 100 injured
15 August 1872	9 days	5 deaths; 343
15 August 1880	4 days	2 deaths; 10 injured
3 June 1886	Over 4 months	32 deaths; 371 injured
11 August 1907	4 days	2 deaths; 23 injured

How and why did such a change in community relations take place? As with many questions in history, there is no one simple answer. What we, as historians, must do is consider all of the changes which took place in Belfast during the 19th century and work out how these changes combined to alter the way the two communities lived with one another.

Learning activities

(a) Divide into groups of four.
(b) Study carefully the following changes which occurred during the 19th century in Belfast. Give each change a score between 1 and 10 to show how important your group feel this change was in altering the attitude of one community to the other community.
   (1 = unimportant   10 = very important).
(c) Write one sentence explaining the reason for each score.

Change No. 1

Belfast was the fastest growing city in the United Kingdom during the second half of the 19th century. The following tables shows the growth in population during this period.

YEAR	POPULATION
1801	19,000
1811	27,832
1821	37,277
1831	53,287
1841	70,447
1851	87,062
1861	121,602
1871	174,412
1881	208,122
1891	255,950
1901	349,180

Change No. 2

As the population of Belfast increased, so did the proportion of the population which was Roman Catholic. The following table shows the percentage of Roman Catholics in the population of Belfast over this period.

YEAR	NO. OF ROMAN CATHOLICS	% OF ROMAN CATHOLICS IN TOTAL POPULATION
1784	1,092	8
1808	4,000	16
1834	19,712	32
1861	41,406	33.9
1871	55,575	31.9
1881	59,975	28.8
1891	67,378	26.3
1901	84,992	24.3

Change No. 3

The following table shows that the increasing population came mainly from the countryside around Belfast and the rest of Ulster.

Birthplaces of Belfast Population 1841-1901				
	1841	1861	1881	1901
Antrim, Down or Belfast City	84.8%	75.2%	77.3%	76.7%
Rest of Ulster	10.5%	15.8%	13.8%	12.6%
Rest of Ireland	2.1%	3.3%	3.05%	3.24%
England, Wales and Scotland	2.36%	5.14%	5.17%	6.64%
Abroad	0.23%	0.57%	0.74%	0.83%

Change No. 4

At the end of the 18th century, relations between the two communities in the countryside were much more troubled than in Belfast. In 1795, after a pitched battle between Catholics and Protestants at the Diamond in Co. Armagh, the Orange Order was founded to protect Protestant interests against Catholic groups such as the Defenders or the Ribbonmen.

The Orange Order established lodges in Belfast in the early 19th century.

Change No. 5

Catholic political movements of the early 19th century, led by Daniel O'Connell, demonstrated the growing power and confidence of the Catholic population which sought the right to vote in elections.

Cartoon of Daniel
O'Connell's visit to Belfast
in 1841.
Ulster Museum
1F/841/O'Connnell.

Change No. 6

There was a growth of evangelical Protestantism in Belfast, beginning in the 1830s
and led by ministers such as Dr Cooke and Rev. Drew, which encouraged the belief
that 'Popery' was an evil influence.

Change No. 7

Belfast changed from a market town and port to an industrial town. Belfast was the
only part of Ireland to experience industrialisation.

Change No. 8

Most industries and businesses were owned by Protestants. Among the working
classes, skilled workers tended to be Protestant while lower-paid unskilled jobs tended
to be filled by Catholics.

Change No. 9

In 1886, there was an attempt to pass a Home Rule Bill, which would have created a
Parliament in Dublin to rule over Ireland. Inevitably, this Dublin parliament would
have had a Catholic majority.

Change No. 10

Businessmen in Belfast feared that Home Rule would lead to a loss of trade with
Britain and the Empire. When asked if Harland and Wolff would move to the Clyde if
Home Rule was passed, the manager of the shipyard, William Pirrie replied: 'Most
certainly this would be done.'

Working class Protestants also feared Home Rule. One Protestant navvy was expelled
from working in the docks by Catholics who told him that once Home Rule was
passed: '...none of the Orange sort would get leave to work or earn a loaf of bread in
Belfast.'

Learning activities

(a) Nominate a spokesperson for your group.

(b) The spokesperson should report back to the rest of the class your scores out of 10 for each change. The spokesperson must be ready to justify each score.

(c) The scores of the different groups should be recorded on the blackboard

(d) There should now follow a general discussion in class with the teacher acting as chairperson. Points to consider should include:

    (i) Which of the changes was most important in leading to a breakdown in community relations?

    (ii) Should these changes be examined separately or in combination with each other?

    (iii) Could anything have been done to improve community relations during the 19th century?

    (iv) Are any of these changes still relevant to the situation to-day?

Concluding Work

Q1 Draw a timeline 1800-1900 listing events of the period in history of Belfast.

Q2 Compare this timeline with the timeline for 1200-1800 drawn at the end of Chapter 1:

    (a) Has the rate of change remained the same in both timelines?

    (b) Can you give any reasons why the rate of change is different?

    (c) Was Belfast alone in experiencing these changes?